Favourite
CASSEROLES
& ONE-POTS

KÖNEMANN

Casseroles

Always warm and welcoming, casseroles can be either a simple, economical everyday affair or can be dressed up with wine and other fine ingredients to become the centrepiece of a casual dinner party. The recipes in this chapter are suitable for summer as well as cold weather — simply serve with a crisp salad and crusty bread instead of hot vegetables.

Apricot Chicken Casserole

Preparation time:
  20 minutes
Total cooking time:
  50 minutes
Serves 4

4 *chicken breast fillets*
  (approximately
  750 g in total)
1/4 *cup flour,*
  seasoned with
  salt and pepper
1 *tablespoon oil*
1 *medium onion,*
  cut into wedges
1 *tablespoon French*
  mustard
170 *ml canned*
  apricot nectar
425 *g canned*
  apricot halves,
  drained and juice
  reserved

1 Preheat the oven to moderate 180°C. Toss chicken in seasoned flour. Heat oil in heavy-based pan. Cook the chicken quickly over medium-high heat until well browned; drain on paper towels.
2 Add onion to pan. Cook for 1 minute or until soft. Place chicken and onions in a 10-cup capacity casserole dish.
3 Mix together French mustard, apricot nectar and reserved apricot juice. Pour over the chicken. Cover with a tight-fitting lid and bake for 30 minutes.
4 Stir in apricot halves. Cook, uncovered, for 10 minutes or until chicken is cooked. Serve Apricot Chicken Casserole with pasta and a green vegetable.

Apricot Chicken Casserole (top) and
Chicken with Champagne and Tarragon

Chicken with Champagne and Tarragon

Preparation time:
  30 minutes
Total cooking time:
  1 hour 15 minutes
Serves 4

1.6 kg chicken
2 cups fresh brown
  breadcrumbs
1 egg, lightly beaten
2 cloves garlic, crushed
2 teaspoons finely
  grated lemon rind
1 tablespoon finely
  chopped fresh tarragon
2 cups champagne or
  dry white wine
1 cup chicken stock
4 whole peppercorns
1 bay leaf

1 Preheat the oven to moderate 180°C. Wash and pat dry chicken. Tuck wing tips to underside. Mix together breadcrumbs, egg, garlic, lemon rind and tarragon. Stuff chicken cavity until almost full. Secure cavity with a skewer. Tie chicken legs together with string.
2 Place chicken breast-side up in an 8-cup capacity casserole dish. Mix together wine and stock and pour over chicken. Add the peppercorns and bay leaf to casserole.

3 Bake, uncovered, for 1¹/4 hours or until chicken is golden and cooked.
4 Place chicken on a serving plate. Cut into pieces, keep warm. Strain sauce and serve with chicken. Serve with steamed asparagus and baby carrots.

Creamy Chicken Marsala

Preparation time:
  20 minutes
Total cooking time:
  1 hour 10 minutes
Serves 4

1 kg chicken thigh
  fillets
¹/4 cup plain flour
2 tablespoons oil
1 onion, sliced
200 g button
  mushrooms, sliced
¹/2 cup chicken stock
¹/2 cup Marsala
250 g Brussels sprouts,
  cleaned and halved
1 carrot, sliced
¹/4 cup cream

1 Preheat the oven to 180°C. Trim chicken of all fat and cut into chunks. Coat chicken in flour; shake off excess. Using half the oil, cook chicken in batches until golden brown. Drain on paper towels. Place into a 12-cup capacity

casserole dish. Heat remaining oil, add onion and mushrooms. Cook for 4-5 minutes or until softened. Add to the chicken.
2 Add chicken stock and Marsala to the pan. Bring to the boil and simmer for 5 minutes. Add to casserole with Brussels sprouts and carrot. Stir through. Cover and cook for 35 minutes. Add cream and cook uncovered for a further 10 minutes.

Garlic and Lamb Casserole

Preparation time:
  30 minutes
Total cooking time:
  2 hours 15 minutes
Serves 4–6

1¹/2 kg lamb neck
  chops
¹/4 cup plain flour
1 tablespoon oil
1 cup beef stock
1 cup red wine
2 carrots, sliced
2 onions, cut into
  wedges
300 g swede, cut into
  chunks
1 small parsnip (300 g),
  cut into chunks
3 celery sticks, sliced
1 tablespoon chopped
  fresh thyme
1 tablespoon chopped
  fresh rosemary

Creamy Chicken Marsala (top) and Garlic and Lamb Casserole

Topping
1 small bread stick
50 g butter
2 cloves garlic, crushed
*1 tablespoon finely
   chopped fresh parsley*

1 Preheat the oven to
180°C. Coat lamb in
flour, shaking off
excess. Heat oil; brown
chops in batches. Drain
on paper towels. Place
into a large, deep
casserole dish.
2 Add stock and wine
to the pan, bring to the
boil and pour over
chops. Add carrots,
onions, swede, parsnip,
celery and herbs to the
casserole. Cover and
bake for 1¹/₂ hours,
stirring twice.

3 To make Topping:
Cut the bread stick into
thick slices. Combine
the butter, garlic and
parsley. Spread bread
with garlic butter.
4 Remove the lid from
the casserole and top
with the garlic bread.
Bake for a further
20–30 minutes or until
bread is golden.

Sausage and Potato Casserole

Preparation time:
  15 minutes
Total cooking time:
  1 hour 10 minutes
Serves 4

2 teaspoons oil
8 thick garlic and herb
  (or plain) sausages
1 onion, sliced
1/4 cup tomato sauce
1 tablespoon
  Worcestershire sauce
1/2 cup beef stock
2 carrots, sliced
1 cup frozen peas
2 fresh tomatoes,
  chopped

Topping
1 kg potatoes, peeled
  and chopped
1/2 cup cream
60 g butter
100 g grated Cheddar
  cheese

1 Preheat the oven to 180°C. Heat oil in a large frying pan. Add sausages and onion. Cook until sausages are golden brown and onion soft. Remove and drain on paper towels. Slice cooled sausages into 3 cm slices and place in a 10-cup capacity casserole dish.

2 Combine tomato sauce, Worcestershire sauce and stock. Add to sausages and onions with carrots. Cover and place in preheated oven. Cook 30 minutes. Add the peas and tomatoes and cook, uncovered, for a further 10 minutes.
3 To make Topping: Steam, microwave or boil the potatoes until tender. Mash until smooth. Mix through the cream and butter. Spoon potato topping on top of casserole. Sprinkle with grated cheese. Return to oven for 10–15 minutes or until cheese has melted.

Spicy Pork and Potato Casserole

Preparation time:
  20 minutes
Total cooking time:
  1 hour 15 minutes
Serves 4–6

1 kg cubed pork
2 tablespoons plain
  flour
2 tablespoons ghee or
  oil
2 teaspoons cumin
1 teaspoon coriander
1 teaspoon garam
  masala
1/2 teaspoon turmeric
1 onion, finely chopped
2 potatoes, cut into
  chunks
1 large sweet potato,
  cut into chunks
11/4 cups beef stock

1 Preheat the oven to 180°C. Coat pork in flour, shake off excess. Heat ghee or oil in a heavy-based pan. Fry pork in small batches, cooking until golden brown. Remove and drain on paper towel. Place into a 10–12-cup capacity casserole dish.
2 Add the spices and onion to pan, cook for 4–5 minutes, or until onion is soft. Add to pork with potato, sweet potato and stock. Stir until well combined.
3 Cook for 1 hour or until pork is tender. Garnish with fresh coriander, if desired.

Hint
Suitable cuts of meat to use in casseroles and hotpots:
Beef: Chuck, blade, silverside, skirt, cubed neck or leg.
Pork: Hand, blade, loin chops, cubed leg and neck.
Veal: Flank, cubed neck or shoulder.
Lamb: Middle neck, chump, breast, cubed shoulder and leg.

Sausage and Potato Casserole (top) and
Spicy Pork and Potato Casserole

Italian Lamb Casserole

Italian Lamb Casserole

Preparation time:
  40 minutes
Total cooking time:
  1 hour 15 minutes
Serves 6

1.5 kg leg lamb, boned
  (ask your butcher
  to do this)
1/2 cup plain flour
1 tablespoon olive oil
30 g butter
4 medium celery sticks,
  sliced diagonally
2 medium carrots,
  sliced diagonally

2 large onions, sliced
2 cloves garlic, crushed
440 g canned tomatoes,
  crushed
1/4 cup tomato paste
1 cup dry white wine
1 cup chicken stock
3/4 teaspoon ground
  oregano
3/4 teaspoon dried
  thyme leaves
1/2 teaspoon dried
  rosemary leaves
black pepper, to taste

1 Preheat the oven to
moderate 180°C. Trim
meat of fat and sinew.
Cut into 4 cm cubes.
Toss meat lightly in
flour; shake off excess.

Heat oil and butter in a
heavy-based pan. Cook
meat quickly in small
batches over medium-
high heat until well
browned. Place in a 10-
cup capacity casserole.
2 Add celery, carrots,
onion and garlic to
pan. Pour in tomatoes
with juice, and stir in
tomato paste. Add
wine, stock and herbs.
Bring to boil, scraping
browned residue from
surface of pan. Pour
over lamb. Season
lightly with pepper.`
3 Cover tightly and
bake for 1 hour, or
until lamb is tender.

Osso Bucco

Osso Bucco

Preparation time:
  30 minutes
Total cooking time:
  2 hours
Serves 6

18 osso bucco (2 kg)
  (veal shanks, cut into
  4 cm pieces)
2¹/4 cups plain flour
¹/4 cup olive oil
1 large onion, chopped
2 cloves garlic, crushed
1 large carrot, sliced
²/3 cup dry white wine
²/3 cup beef stock
440 g canned tomatoes
¹/4 cup tomato paste
¹/2 teaspoon caster
  sugar

Gremolata
¹/3 cup parsley sprigs
1 clove garlic, crushed
2 teaspoons grated
  lemon rind

1 Preheat the oven to
moderate 180°C.
Lightly grease a 12-cup
capacity baking dish.
Toss osso bucco lightly
in seasoned flour; shake
off excess.
2 Heat a little of the oil
in a heavy-based pan.
Cook meat quickly on
both sides over
medium-high heat until

well browned; drain on
paper towels. Transfer
meat to baking dish.
3 Add onion, garlic and
carrot to pan, stir until
onion is soft. Add the
wine, stock, undrained
chopped tomatoes,
tomato paste and sugar.
Bring to boil; reduce
heat; simmer 5 minutes.
4 Spoon sauce over
meat. Cover dish with
foil, bake for 1³/4 hours
or until meat is tender.
5 To make Gremolata:
Finely chop the parsley
sprigs and combine
with the garlic and
lemon rind. Sprinkle
over Osso Bucco.

9

Lamb and Mushroom Casserole

Preparation time:
  20 minutes
Total cooking time:
  2 hours 15 minutes
Serves 4

4 large lamb leg chops,
  (about 175 g each)
1 tablespoon oil
440 g canned cream of
  mushroom soup
1 tablespoon
  Worcestershire sauce
3/4 cup chicken stock
1/2 cup dry sherry
2 teaspoons oil, extra
250 g button
  mushrooms, sliced
2 large onions, sliced

1 Preheat the oven to moderate 180°C. Trim chops of excess fat and sinew. Heat oil in a heavy-based pan. Cook chops for 1 minute on either side or until well browned; drain on paper towels.
2 Place chops in an 8-cup capacity casserole dish. Mix together soup, Worcestershire sauce, chicken stock and sherry. Pour over the chops. Cover casserole and bake for 1¹/2 hours.

3 Heat extra oil in a pan and cook the button mushrooms for 3 minutes, or until brown. Set aside. Add onions to pan and cook for 5 minutes, or until soft and golden.
4 Stir mushrooms through the casserole. Sprinkle onion slices over casserole. Return to oven, uncovered, for 30 minutes, or until onions are crisp and lamb is tender. Serve casserole with steamed fresh vegetables.

Meatballs with Tomatoes and Artichokes

Preparation time:
  30 minutes
Total cooking time:
  1 hour
Serves 4

750 g minced beef
2 cloves garlic, crushed
2 tablespoons finely
  chopped fresh basil
1 egg, lightly beaten
1/2 cup fresh
  breadcrumbs
2 tablespoons oil
425 g canned peeled
  tomatoes, crushed
2 tablespoons tomato
  paste

1/4 cup red wine
1/2 teaspoon ground
  oregano
1/4 cup beef stock
400 g canned
  chickpeas, drained
425 g canned artichoke
  hearts, drained and
  quartered
1/3 cup pitted black
  olives

1 Preheat the oven to moderate 180°C. Combine mince, garlic, basil, beaten egg and breadcrumbs. Mix well. Roll tablespoons of mixture into balls.
2 Heat half the oil in a heavy-based pan. Cook half of the meatballs for 4 minutes, turning occasionally until brown; drain on paper towels. Repeat process with the other half of the meatballs. Place meatballs in an 8-cup capacity casserole dish.
3 Mix together the crushed tomatoes, tomato paste, red wine, oregano and beef stock. Pour the mixture over the meatballs in the casserole dish.
4 Cover and bake for 40 minutes. Add the chickpeas, artichoke hearts and pitted black olives. Bake meatballs, uncovered, for a further 5 minutes, or until they are heated through. Serve with roasted eggplant slices.

Lamb and Mushroom Casserole (top) and Meatballs with Tomatoes and Artichokes

1. *For Beef and Herb Puff Casserole: Brown meat quickly in small batches.*

2. *Place browned meat and chopped onions in a casserole dish.*

Beef and Herb Puff Casserole

Preparation time:
  20 minutes
Total cooking time:
  2 hours 20 minutes
Serves 4–6

1 kg chuck steak
2 tablespoons oil
1/2 cup seasoned flour
2 onions, chopped
1 1/2 cups beef stock
2 tablespoons
  Worcestershire sauce
1 tablespoon soy sauce
2 small carrots, finely
  chopped
1 green capsicum, finely
  chopped

Herb Puffs
1 cup self-raising flour
60 g butter, chopped
2–3 tablespoons milk
1 tablespoon finely
  chopped fresh parsley
1 tablespoon finely
  chopped fresh thyme
1 tablespoon finely
  chopped chives
1/3 cup grated Cheddar
  cheese

1 Preheat the oven to moderate 180°C. Trim the meat of excess fat and sinew and cut into 4 cm cubes. Toss the meat lightly in flour; shake off excess. Heat half the oil in a heavy-based pan. Cook the meat quickly in small batches over medium-high heat for 4 minutes or until well browned; drain on paper towels.
2 Heat the remaining oil in the pan. Cook the onions for 2 minutes or until brown; drain on paper towels. Place the meat and onions in an 8-cup casserole dish.
3 Mix together the beef stock, Worcestershire sauce and soy sauce. Pour over the beef and onions. Cover the casserole and bake for 1 3/4 hours, adding the carrot and capsicum during the last 30 minutes of cooking.
4 To make Herb Puffs: Place the flour in a bowl. Using your fingertips, rub the butter into the flour until the mixture is a fine, crumbly texture. Add the milk, herbs and cheese; stir. Turn the dough onto a lightly floured surface. Knead for 2 minutes or until smooth. Pull dough apart into rough balls.
5 Remove the casserole from the oven. Place the herb rounds on top of the casserole. Brush the tops with a little extra milk and bake the casserole, uncovered, for 15 minutes or until the Herb Puffs are puffed and golden.

Beef and Herb Puff Casserole

3. Pull the kneaded and rolled Herb Puff dough apart into rough balls.

4. Place the Herb Puffs on top of the casserole and return to oven.

Irish Braise

Preparation time:
  10 minutes
Total cooking time:
  1 hour 45 minutes
Serves 4

1 kg chuck steak
2 tablespoons oil
3 rashers bacon,
  chopped
2 large carrots, sliced
8 small onions, halved
185 g button
  mushrooms, see Note
1 teaspoon dried thyme
  leaves
2 tablespoons plain
  flour
3/4 cup dry white wine
3/4 cup beef stock

1 Preheat the oven to moderate 180°C. Trim meat of excess fat and sinew and cut in 2 cm cubes. Heat oil in a heavy-based pan. Cook meat quickly in small batches over medium-high heat until well browned; drain on paper towels.
2 Add bacon to pan. Cook over medium heat until browned; drain on paper towels.
3 Place meat and bacon in a 6-cup capacity casserole dish with carrots, onions, mushrooms and thyme.
4 Mix together flour, wine and stock; stir until smooth. Pour over meat and vegetables. Cover and bake for 1 1/2 hours, or until meat is tender. Serve with rice.

Note: Substitute field mushrooms, sliced, if button mushrooms are unavailable.

Sailor's Stew

Preparation time:
  10 minutes
Total cooking time:
  2 hours 10 minutes
Serves 8–10

1.5 kg chuck steak
1/2 cup plain flour
2 tablespoons
  vegetable oil
30 g butter
4 large potatoes, peeled
  and sliced thickly,
  see Note
4 onions, sliced
2 large carrots, sliced
  thickly (optional)
1 teaspoon whole black
  peppercorns
3 cups beer
2 cups beef stock
2 tablespoons soy sauce
2 or 3 bay leaves

1 Preheat the oven to moderate 180°C. Trim meat of excess fat and sinew and cut in 2 cm cubes. Toss meat lightly in flour; shake off the excess. Heat the oil and butter in a heavy-based pan. Cook the meat quickly in small batches until well browned; drain on paper towels.
2 Arrange potatoes in the bottom of a deep 14-cup capacity casserole dish. Place the meat, onions and carrots on top, and sprinkle with black peppercorns. Pour in the beer, beef stock and soy sauce, and add the bay leaves.
3 Bake, uncovered, for 2 hours, or until meat is tender. Serve with crusty bread.

Note: Use old, floury potatoes, as they break down during cooking and thicken the sauce.

HINT
For an unusual and delicious variation, serve tomato-based or spicy casseroles over couscous. This grain, from the Middle East, is made from wheat and is delicious and simple to prepare. Instant couscous is available in packets from delicatessens. It just needs soaking in stock or water.

Sailor's Stew (top) and Irish Braise

Spicy Bean Casserole

Preparation time:
  20 minutes
Total cooking time:
  45 minutes
Serves 4

750 g canned 4-bean
  mix
oil, for frying
1 onion, finely chopped
1 clove garlic, crushed
2 teaspoons cumin
1/2 teaspoon cayenne
  pepper
1/2 teaspoon chilli
  powder
1 carrot, diced
1 red capsicum, diced
425 g canned tomatoes,
  chopped
1/2 cup vegetable stock

1 Preheat the oven
moderate 180°C
4-bean mix a
well; set asid
2 Heat a li
frying pa
and garl
2 minut
Stir in cu
and chill
for 2 mi
mixture i
3 Place on
in an 8-cup
casserole dis
carrot, capsic
tomatoes, stoc
4-bean mix. Co
40 minutes. Seas
with salt and pepp

Potato and Pumpkin Casserole

Preparation time:
  25 minutes
Total cooking time:
  50 minutes
Serves 4

950 g potatoes
700 g pumpkin
2 tablespoons butter
1 large onion, chopped
1 tablespoon plain flour
1/2 cup cream
3/4 cup milk
1/2 cup grated
  Parmes
1 cu
ch

heat; bring slowly to
the boil, stirring
constantly, until it boils
and thickens. Season
with salt and pepper.
Stir in cooked onion.
3 Pour sauce over the
vegetables. Sprinkle
combined cheese over
the top. Bake for
30 minutes or until
golden brown.

Lentil and Vegetable Casserole

Preparation time:
  25 minutes + 2 hours
  soaking
cooking time:
  minutes

Clockwise from top left: Spicy Bean Casserole, Potato and Pumpkin Casserole, Lentil and Vegetable Casserole

425 g *canned tomatoes, chopped*
2 tablespoons *tomato paste*

1 Soak lentils in cold water for 2 hours, then rinse and drain well. Preheat the oven to moderate 180°C.

2 Heat oil in frying pan; add the leek and garlic and cook for 3 minutes or until soft. Add the ground paprika and oregano and cook for 2 minutes or until fragrant.
3 Place in a 10-cup capacity casserole dish

along with the celery, zucchini, capsicum, eggplant, potatoes, vegetable stock, canned tomatoes and tomato paste. Cover and cook casserole for 1 1/2 hours, stirring occasionally. Season well with salt and pepper.

17

Hotpots and Pot Roasts

Every national cuisine has wonderful, cooked-in-one-pot dishes which can be put together with a minimum of fuss yet give maximum flavour and take advantage of economical seasonal ingredients. One-pot dishes fit perfectly into a busy, modern-day schedule, and are a great way to feed a crowd. Most are best made at least a day ahead, allowing flavours to mingle and develop beautifully. Always store, covered, in the refrigerator. Pot roasts are at their best served straight from the stove to the table.

Herbed Beef Roast

Preparation time:
  10 minutes
Total cooking time:
  1 hour 10 minutes
Serves 4–6

1.5 kg topside roast
1 tablespoon oil
8 sprigs fresh parsley
8 sprigs fresh
  rosemary
8 sprigs fresh basil
8 sprigs fresh thyme
8 pickling onions
1 cup water
420 g canned beef
  consommé
1 cup red wine
2 teaspoons cornflour
1 tablespoon water,
  extra

1 Trim meat of excess fat. Heat oil in a deep heavy-based pan, add meat and cook over medium-high heat until well browned. Remove pan from heat.
2 Arrange herbs and onions around meat. Gently pour in water, consommé and wine. Return to heat, reduce heat to low. Cover and bring to simmering point. Simmer 1 hour, turning occasionally. Remove meat from pan, cover, keep warm.
3 Add combined cornflour and extra water to liquid. Bring to boil and simmer for 10 minutes. Strain.
4 Slice meat and serve with sauce and onions.

Herbed Beef Roast (top) and Chilli Coconut Beef

Chilli Coconut Beef

Preparation time:
 30 minutes
Total cooking time:
 1 hour 15 minutes
Serves 2–4

500 g blade steak
1 tablespoon oil
8 spring onions,
 chopped
2 teaspoons grated
 ginger
2 red chillies, seeded
 and chopped
1 clove garlic, chopped
2 teaspoons finely
 grated lemon rind
1 teaspoon lemon juice
4 tablespoons
 desiccated coconut
1 tablespoon oil, extra
1¹/2 cups water
1 cup coconut milk
1 teaspoon sugar
freshly ground black
 pepper, to taste

1 Trim meat of excess fat and sinew and cut in 2 cm cubes. Heat oil in a heavy-based pan. Cook meat quickly in small batches over medium-high heat until well browned; drain on paper towels.
2 Mix spring onion, ginger, chilli, garlic, lemon rind and juice in a bowl and set aside.
3 Cook coconut in a dry pan over medium heat, stirring constantly, until golden brown. Remove from pan.
4 Heat extra oil in same pan. Add spring onion mixture and cook for 5 minutes. Add coconut and cook for 1 minute.
5 Add meat, water, coconut milk, sugar and pepper to taste. Bring to boil, reduce heat and simmer, uncovered, for 1 hour or until meat is tender, stirring occasionally. Serve with boiled or steamed rice.

Note: The sauce should reduce to a very thick coating over the meat.

Creamy Peppercorn Stew

Preparation time:
 30 minutes
Total cooking time:
 1 hour 10 minutes
Serves 4–6

750 g chuck steak
2 tablespoons plain
 flour
2 tablespoons oil
20 g butter
3 small onions, cut in
 wedges
1 celery stick, sliced
1 tablespoon canned
 green peppercorns,
 drained
¹/2 teaspoon ground
 allspice
1 large carrot, sliced
2 medium parsnips,
 peeled and sliced
2 cups beef stock
¹/2 cup cream

1 Trim meat of excess fat and sinew and cut in 2 cm cubes. Toss lightly in flour; shake off excess. Heat oil and butter in large heavy-based pan. Cook meat quickly in small batches over medium-high heat until well browned.
2 Return meat to pan with onions, celery, peppercorns, allspice, carrot, parsnips and stock; bring to the boil. Reduce heat and simmer, covered, 1 hour or until meat is tender. Remove from heat, stir through cream and serve with pasta and a green salad.

Tex Mex Beef

Preparation time:
 25 minutes
Total cooking time:
 1 hour 20 minutes
Serves 6

1 kg chuck steak
1 tablespoon oil
2 tablespoons plain
 flour
1 teaspoon Mexican-
 style chilli powder
2 cloves garlic,
 chopped

Creamy Peppercorn Stew (top) and Tex Mex Beef

1 teaspoon ground
  cumin
1 teaspoon dried
  oregano leaves
pinch cayenne pepper
3 cups beef stock
1/4 cup tomato sauce
1 tablespoon red wine
  vinegar
425 g canned red
  kidney beans, drained
sour cream
corn chips

1 Trim meat of excess fat and sinew and cut into 1 cm cubes. Heat oil in a deep, heavy-based pan. Cook meat quickly, in small batches, over medium-high heat until well browned; drain on paper towels.
2 Return meat to pan with the flour, chilli powder, garlic, cumin, oregano and cayenne pepper to taste and stir for 3 minutes.

3 Remove pan from heat, add stock, tomato sauce and vinegar and mix well. Return to heat, bring to the boil, stirring. Reduce heat and simmer, uncovered, 45 minutes to 1 hour or until beef is tender, stirring occasionally.
4 Stir through the red kidney beans, cook for 2 minutes. Serve with a dollop of sour cream and corn chips.

21

1. For Italian Beef Pot Roast: Pour the combined marinade over meat.

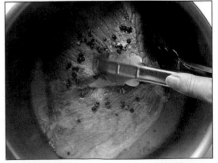

2. Add meat to pan, cook over medium-high heat until well browned.

Italian Beef Pot Roast

Preparation time:
  30 minutes + 4 hours
  standing
Total cooking time:
  1 hour 40 minutes
Serves 4–6

1.5 kg piece silverside
2 cups white vinegar
2 cloves garlic, crushed
1 sprig fresh thyme
1 teaspoon whole black
  peppercorns
1 tablespoon olive oil
1 cup red wine
2 tablespoons soft
  brown sugar
1/2 cup beef stock
2 tablespoons balsamic
  vinegar
440 g canned tomato
  puree
1 eggplant, chopped
1/3 cup pitted black
  olives

440 g canned artichoke
  hearts, drained
  and halved

1 Trim meat of excess
fat. Mix together white
vinegar, garlic, thyme
and peppercorns. Pour
over meat. Store,
covered with plastic
wrap, in refrigerator for
4 hours, turning
occasionally. Drain and
discard marinade. Pat
silverside dry with
paper towels.
2 Heat oil in a deep,
heavy-based pan, add
meat, cook over a
medium-high heat until
meat is well browned
on all sides.
3 Remove pan from
heat. Add wine, sugar,
stock, vinegar and
tomato puree, return to
heat, reduce heat to
low. Cover the pan and
bring casserole slowly
to simmering point.

Simmer for 1 1/4–1 1/2
hours. Turn meat
occasionally, adding
eggplant for the last
30 minutes of cooking.
4 Remove meat from
the pan. Keep warm.
Stir in olives and
artichokes and cook for
2 minutes.
5 Slice meat, serve with
the vegetables, olives
and pan sauce.

HINT
Suitable cuts of meat
for pot roasting are
whole pieces of well-
flavoured and tender
meat. If necessary, ask
your butcher to bone,
trim and tie the meat
for you.
Beef: Topside, rump,
silverside.
Lamb: Leg, shoulder,
shank.
Veal: Shoulder, rolled
breast or middleneck.
Pork: Rolled hand,
rolled neck, hand, leg.

Italian Beef Pot Roast

*3. Add wine, sugar, beef stock, balsamic
vinegar and tomato puree.*

*4. Stir in olives and artichokes; cook for
2 minutes. Serve immediately.*

One-pot Moroccan Lamb

Preparation time:
  5 minutes
Total cooking time:
  1 hour 15 minutes
Serves 4

750 g lean lamb
1 tablespoon oil
2 cups beef or chicken
  stock
2 small onions, chopped
1/2 cup pitted prunes,
  halved
1/2 cup dried apricots,
  halved
1 teaspoon ginger
1 teaspoon cinnamon
black pepper, to taste
1/4 cup toasted slivered
  almonds

1 Trim meat of excess fat and sinew and cut in 2 cm cubes. Heat oil in a large heavy-based pan. Cook the meat quickly, in small batches, over medium-high heat for 2 minutes or until well browned.
2 Add stock, onions, prunes, apricots, ginger, cinnamon and pepper to pan; bring to boil. Reduce heat; simmer, covered, for 1 hour or until meat is tender. Garnish with almonds. Serve with rice.

Note: A boned leg of lamb is suitable.

Indian Lamb Curry

Preparation time:
  20 minutes
Total cooking time:
  30 minutes
Serves 4–6

750 g lamb fillets, cut
  into strips
2 tablespoons seasoned
  flour
2 tablespoons oil
2 medium onions,
  sliced thickly
1 clove garlic, crushed
1 teaspoon grated
  ginger
1 tablespoon curry
  powder
1 teaspoon garam
  masala
1/2 teaspoon mustard
  seeds
300 g cauliflower, cut
  into florets
2 celery sticks, sliced
1 cup beef stock
2 tablespoons freshly
  chopped coriander

1 Toss meat lightly in flour; shake off excess. Heat half the oil in a heavy-based frying pan. Cook meat quickly in small batches over medium-high heat until well browned; drain on paper towels.
2 Heat remaining oil in pan. Cook onions for 2 minutes on medium heat until soft. Stir in the garlic, ginger, curry powder, garam masala and mustard seeds. Cook for 2 minutes or until fragrant.
3 Add the cauliflower, celery and beef stock. Cover and cook for 10 minutes. Stir in lamb strips and cook for a further 5 minutes, uncovered, or until heated through.

Tomato Lamb Pot Roast

Preparation time:
  10 minutes
Total cooking time:
  2 hours
Serves 6

1.6 kg leg lamb
1 tablespoon oil
440 g canned peeled
  tomatoes, crushed ·
1/2 cup red wine
4 whole black
  peppercorns
1 tablespoon fresh
  rosemary leaves
1 tablespoon
  Worcestershire sauce
1/2 cup beef stock
8 small potatoes, peeled
  and halved
8 slices butternut
  pumpkin
8 Brussels sprouts,
  optional

1 Trim meat of excess fat. Heat oil in a deep, heavy-based pan, add

Clockwise from top: Tomato Lamb Pot Roast, One-pot Moroccan Lamb, Indian Lamb Curry

meat and cook over medium-high heat, turning until the meat is well browned.

2 Remove the pan from heat. Add the tomatoes, wine, peppercorns, rosemary leaves and the Worcestershire sauce and beef stock. Return the pan to the heat and reduce the heat to low.

Cover the pan and simmer for 1½ hours, turning the meat over occasionally.

3 Add the potatoes and pumpkin and simmer for 15 minutes. Add the Brussels sprouts and simmer for 5 minutes. Slice the meat and serve with the vegetables and pan juices.

HINT
Use a pan with a well-fitting lid where necessary. If your pot or casserole lid is loose, cover dish with aluminium foil, press down and then place the lid on top.

25

Spicy Coriander Lamb

Preparation time:
  10 minutes
Total cooking time:
  1 hour 15 minutes
Serves 6

1 kg chump lamb chops
1 tablespoon olive oil
2 small onions, chopped
2 cloves garlic, crushed
1 tablespoon ground
  ginger
1 tablespoon ground
  coriander
2 teaspoons ground
  cumin
1 teaspoon turmeric
freshly ground black
  pepper, to taste
2 cups chicken stock
1/3 cup finely chopped
  fresh coriander

1 Trim meat of excess fat and sinew. Heat oil in a large heavy-based pan. Cook meat quickly, in small batches, over medium-high heat for 2 minutes or until well browned; drain meat on paper towels.
2 Add the onions and garlic to pan. Cook for 2 minutes or until browned. Stir in spices, cook for 1–2 minutes or until fragrant.
3 Return meat to pan with the stock and coriander; bring to the boil. Reduce heat and simmer, covered, for 1 hour or until meat is tender. Serve with steamed or boiled rice and seasonal vegetables.

Farmhouse Chicken Hotpot

Preparation time:
  10 minutes
Total cooking time:
  50 minutes
Serves 4

1 tablespoon oil
500 g chicken thigh
  fillets, cut in halves
1 1/2 cups chicken stock
2 medium carrots,
  sliced
250 g small new
  potatoes, halved
1/2 teaspoon ground
  allspice
2 bay leaves
2 medium leeks, sliced
8 baby squash, halved
1 teaspoon ground
  black pepper
1/3 cup sour cream

1 Heat oil in a large heavy-based pan. Cook the chicken quickly in small batches over medium-high heat until well browned.
2 Add stock, carrots, potatoes, allspice and bay leaves to the pan; bring to the boil. Reduce heat and simmer, covered, for 45 minutes or until chicken is tender.
3 Add the leeks and squash and simmer for 15 minutes.
4 Remove the bay leaves. Stir through the pepper and sour cream. Cook for 1 minute or until heated through. Serve with pasta or crusty bread.

Note: After slicing, wash leeks thoroughly in warm water to remove all grit and dirt from between the layers. Be careful not to overcook the leeks as they become mushy and disintegrate.

HINT
Garlic bread goes well with casseroles and pot roasts. Make diagonal slices in a French loaf and spread with softened butter beaten with chopped parsley and crushed garlic to taste. Wrap the loaf in foil and bake in a moderate oven 180°C until the bread has heated through and the butter melted.

Farmhouse Chicken Hotpot (top) and
Spicy Coriander Lamb

Sweet Chicken Curry

Preparation time:
 20 minutes
Total cooking time:
 40 minutes
Serves 4

*500 g chicken thigh
 fillets*
2 teaspoons oil
*1/3 cup blanched
 almonds*
*1 tablespoon green
 curry paste*
1/4 teaspoon turmeric
*440 g canned pineapple
 pieces in natural juice,
 juice reserved*
1 red capsicum
3 small zucchini
1/3 cup currants

1 Cut chicken in 2 cm cubes. Heat oil in a heavy-based pan, add almonds, curry paste and turmeric. Cook for 2 minutes, stirring; add chicken, stir 5 minutes.
2 Add reserved juice; bring to boil. Reduce heat. Simmer, covered, 20–25 minutes or until chicken is tender.

Clockwise from top left: Spiced Chicken Pot Roast with Brown Rice Pilaf, Quick and Easy Spicy Hotpot, Chicken and Broccoli One-pot, Sweet Chicken Curry

29

1. For Chicken and Broccoli One-pot:
Cook chicken quickly in small batches.

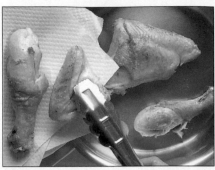

2. Remove from pan and drain on paper
towels.

3 Chop capsicum. Cut zucchini into sticks. Add to pan with pineapple and currants. Simmer, covered, 20–25 minutes or until the vegetables are tender.

Chicken and Broccoli One-pot

Preparation time:
  20 minutes
Total cooking time:
  50 minutes
Serves 4

1 tablespoon oil
1.5 kg chicken pieces
425 g canned tomatoes,
  chopped
1 tablespoon
  Worcestershire sauce
1 teaspoon ground
  cumin
1/4 cup red wine
2 tablespoons tomato
  paste
1/4 teaspoon Tabasco
  sauce

1/2 cup chicken stock
250 g button
  mushrooms, halved
300 g broccoli florets

1 Heat the oil in a large heavy-based pan. Cook chicken pieces quickly, in small batches, over medium-high heat until well browned. Drain the chicken pieces on paper towels and return to the pan.
2 Add the tomatoes, Worcestershire sauce, cumin, wine, tomato paste, Tabasco sauce and stock to the pan; bring to the boil. Reduce heat and simmer, covered, for 35 minutes or until the chicken is tender, stirring occasionally.
3 Stir in the mushrooms and broccoli and simmer, uncovered, for 5 minutes or until the vegetables are cooked. Serve with boiled or steamed rice.

Quick and Easy Spicy Hotpot

Preparation time:
  30 minutes
Total cooking time:
  35 minutes
Serves 6

1 tablespoon olive oil
4 spicy Italian sausages
1 large onion, chopped
1 clove garlic, crushed
1 red capsicum,
  chopped
1 green capsicum,
  chopped
300 g button
  mushrooms, halved
425 g canned tomatoes,
  chopped
1/2 cup dry white wine
1/2 cup chicken stock
1 teaspoon dried
  oregano leaves
1 teaspoon dried
  marjoram
black pepper, to taste
1 large barbecued
  chicken, cut in 8 pieces

3. Add Worcestershire sauce, cumin, wine, tomato paste, Tabasco and stock.

4. Add mushrooms and broccoli to pan, stir, simmer for 5 minutes.

1 Heat half the oil in a large heavy-based pan. Cook sausages quickly over medium-high heat for 5 minutes or until well browned; drain on paper towels. Drain fat from pan.
2 Heat remaining oil and add onion, garlic and capsicum to pan and cook for 5 minutes. Add mushrooms and cook 3 minutes. Slice the sausages diagonally in 2 cm slices.
3 Return sausages to pan with tomatoes, wine, stock, oregano, marjoram and pepper to taste; bring to boil. Reduce heat to simmer and cook, uncovered, 15 minutes, or until liquid is reduced and slightly thickened. Add cooked chicken pieces and simmer 5 minutes, or until heated through. Garnish with chopped fresh parsley if desired; serve with crusty bread.

Spiced Chicken Pot Roast with Brown Rice Pilaf

Preparation time:
  5 minutes
Total cooking time:
  1 hour 40 minutes
Serves 4–6

2 tablespoons vegetable oil
1.5 kg chicken
1/2 cup chicken stock
1 bay leaf
1 clove garlic, crushed
1 tablespoon oil, extra
1 onion, finely chopped
1 1/4 cups brown rice
3 whole cloves
1 teaspoon turmeric
1/2 teaspoon ground cardamom
1 1/2 cups chicken stock
1 1/2 cups water
2 teaspoons tomato paste
black pepper, to taste
3 spring onions, finely chopped

1 Heat oil in a deep, heavy-based pan, add chicken and cook over medium-high heat, turning until well browned on all sides.
2 Remove pan from heat. Add stock, bay leaf and garlic, return to heat, reduce heat to low. Cover and leave to simmer for 20 minutes.
3 Heat extra oil in a medium pan and cook onion until tender. Add rice and spices and stir 2 minutes. Add stock, water, tomato paste and pepper; bring to boil.
4 Pour hot rice and liquid around chicken. Simmer, covered, for 1 hour, or until chicken is tender and rice absorbs all the liquid. Add spring onions after 45 minutes.
5 Remove chicken to cutting board. Cut into serving pieces. Serve on a platter with Brown Rice Pilaf.

Pork and Apple Pot Roast

Preparation time:
  10 minutes
Total cooking time:
  1 hour 50 minutes
Serves 4–6

1.5 kg boned shoulder
  pork (ask your
  butcher to do this)
1 tablespoon oil
³/4 cup chicken stock
2 tablespoons honey
¹/4 teaspoon ground
  cinnamon
³/4 cup apple juice or
  cider
rind of 1 lemon, cut
  into strips
3 apples, peeled, cored
  and cut into eighths

1 Trim meat of excess fat, removing rind if you wish. Tie with string to retain shape. Heat oil in a deep, heavy-based pan, add meat and cook over medium-high heat until well browned on all sides.
2 Remove pan from heat. Add stock, honey, cinnamon, apple juice and lemon rind, return to heat, reduce heat to low. Cover, bring slowly to simmering point, simmer 1 hour 15 minutes, or until meat is tender, turning occasionally.

3 Add apple pieces to pan and simmer for 15–20 minutes, or until apples are very soft and liquid has reduced and thickened.
4 Serve slices of pork with apples and sauce spooned over.

Creamy Lemon Pork

Preparation time:
  20 minutes
Total cooking time:
  45 minutes
Serves 4

750 g pork fillet or
  loin, cut into
  small cubes
50 g butter
185 g button
  mushrooms, sliced
1 cup chicken stock
1 tablespoon plain
  flour
¹/2 cup cream
1 tablespoon lemon
  juice
freshly ground black
  pepper, to taste
¹/2 small lemon, cut
  into small wedges
finely chopped fresh
  parsley

1 Trim meat of excess fat and sinew. Heat half of the butter in a heavy-based pan. Cook

meat quickly, in small batches, over medium-high heat until well browned; drain on paper towels.
2 Heat remaining butter and add mushrooms to pan and cook for 2 minutes. Return meat to pan with stock; bring to boil. Reduce heat to simmer and cook, covered, 30 minutes or until meat is tender, stirring occasionally.
3 Mix together flour and cream. Add to pan, increase heat and stir until sauce thickens. Simmer for 2 minutes. Season with lemon juice and black pepper. Serve decorated with the lemon wedges and fresh parsley.

HINT
Brown whole cuts of meat slowly for deep caramelisation. This gives a better flavour to pot roasts as well as sealing in juices. Simmering over gentle heat is vital to break down tough tissue. If allowed to boil, the meat will remain tough — bring to simmering, rather than boiling, point.

Pork and Apple Pot Roast (top) and
Creamy Lemon Pork

Red Pork Curry

Preparation time:
  10 minutes
Total cooking time:
  25 minutes
Serves 6

1 tablespoon oil
2–4 teaspoons red chilli
  paste
500 g boneless lean
  pork, cut in thin
  strips
1 cup coconut milk
1 medium eggplant, cut
  in small cubes
1/2 cup sliced canned
  bamboo shoots,
  drained
10–15 fresh basil leaves
2 dried kaffir lime
  leaves, optional
2 tablespoons fish
  sauce
extra fresh basil leaves
  or strips of seeded
  fresh red chillies

1 Heat oil in a heavy-based pan, cook chilli paste over medium heat for 1–2 minutes, stirring constantly, until fragrant. Add pork and stir for 5 minutes or until meat is well browned.
2 Add coconut milk, eggplant, bamboo shoots, basil leaves, lime leaves, if using, and fish sauce; bring to the boil. Reduce heat to simmer and cook, covered, for 15 minutes or until meat is tender, stirring occasionally.
3 Garnish with basil or red chillies and serve with steamed rice.

Country Sausage Hotpot

Preparation time:
  10 minutes
Total cooking time:
  30 minutes
Serves 4

8–10 thin pork
  sausages
2 teaspoons oil
2 small leeks, sliced
440 g canned tomato
  puree
1/4 cup water
2 tablespoons red wine
2 medium carrots,
  thinly sliced
2 celery sticks, thinly
  sliced
2 tablespoons finely
  chopped fresh parsley

1 Preheat grill. Pierce sausages all over with a fork; cook sausages under medium heat for 6 minutes or until cooked, turning often. Drain on paper towels. Cut sausages in half.

*Country Sausage Hotpot (top) and
Red Pork Curry*

2 Heat oil in a heavy-based pan. Add leeks and cook, stirring, for 3 minutes or until soft. Add the tomato puree, water, wine, carrots and celery; bring to boil. Reduce heat and simmer, uncovered, for 5 minutes, stirring occasionally.
3 Return sausages to pan. Simmer 2 minutes or until sausages are heated through and vegetables are tender. Stir through parsley Serve with mashed potatoes or boiled rice.

Ratatouille

Preparation time:
 10 minutes
Total cooking time:
 30 minutes
Serves 6

2 tablespoons olive oil
2 medium onions, cut in wedges
2 medium zucchini, cut in thick sticks
1 small red capsicum, sliced
1 small green capsicum, sliced
1 small yellow capsicum, sliced
2 cloves garlic, crushed
1 medium eggplant, cubed
440 g canned tomatoes, crushed

freshly ground black pepper to taste
1/2 teaspoon dried basil or oregano leaves
1 tablespoon fresh parsley

1 Heat oil in a large, heavy-based pan and cook the onion over medium heat 4 minutes or until soft. Add zucchini, capsicum and garlic, stir 3 minutes.
2 Add eggplant to pan with tomatoes, pepper and basil or oregano; bring to boil. Reduce heat to simmer, cook, covered, 15 minutes or until vegetables are tender. Sprinkle with parsley and serve with crusty bread.

Vegetable Curry

Preparation time:
 10 minutes
Total cooking time:
 40 minutes
Serves 6

1 tablespoon oil
2 onions, chopped
1 tablespoon grated fresh ginger
2 cloves garlic, crushed
2 teaspoons curry powder
2 teaspoons green curry paste

1 teaspoon ground cumin
880 g canned tomatoes, crushed
1/4 cup tomato paste
1/2 cup sweet fruit chutney
1/4 cup crunchy peanut butter
440 ml canned coconut cream
375 g pumpkin, chopped
1 medium carrot, chopped
125 g fresh beans, sliced into 4 cm lengths
125 g yellow or green squash, chopped
125 g cauliflower florets
2 medium potatoes, peeled and chopped
310 g canned butter beans

1 Heat oil in a large, heavy-based pan. Cook the onions, ginger and garlic over medium heat for 3 minutes. Stir in curry powder, paste and ground cumin and cook for 2 minutes or until fragrant.
2 Add all of the remaining ingredients and stir to combine; bring to boil. Reduce heat to simmer and cook, covered, for 30 minutes, stirring occasionally. Serve with steamed rice.

Vegetable Curry (top) and Ratatouille

Quick and Easy

For many cooks today, time is of the essence. These recipes have their base in Italy, Spain or France, where clever cooks have always taken sensible short cuts in the kitchen. Based on the classic time-savers of rice, eggs and pasta, they lose nothing in flavour. Ready-to-cook ingredients such as bottled pesto and canned tomatoes stretch your time even further. And one-pot preparation means less time at the sink and more time relaxing at the table.

Penne with Creamy Pesto and Tomato

Preparation time:
  5 minutes
Total cooking time:
  20 minutes
Serves 4

375 g penne pasta
2 teaspoons oil
200 g mushrooms,
  sliced
3/4 cup sour cream
1/2 cup bottled pesto
1/3 cup chopped
  sun-dried tomatoes
black pepper to taste

1 Cook the pasta, in a large pan of rapidly boiling water with a little oil added, until just tender; drain.
2 Return pan to heat, add oil. When hot, add mushrooms and cook 4 minutes or until soft and golden. Stir in sour cream, pesto, tomatoes and pepper. Mix well and cook for 2 minutes or until the sauce is heated through.
3 Return pasta to pan and mix well. Cook, stirring, 1 minute or until heated through. Serve immediately with crusty bread.

Note: Pesto can be bought in jars from supermarkets and delicatessens, or can be made at home. (See recipe page 61.)

Smoked Salmon Spirals (top) and Penne with Creamy Pesto and Tomato

Smoked Salmon Spirals

Preparation time:
  10 minutes
Total cooking time:
  15 minutes
Serves 4

375 g small pasta spirals
1/4 cup lemon juice
1 cup light sour cream
1/4 cup cream
6 slices smoked salmon
  (100 g), chopped
2 tablespoons finely
  chopped fresh chives
1/3 cup toasted slivered
  almonds

1 Cook the pasta in a large pan of rapidly boiling water until just tender; drain.
2 Return pan to heat, add lemon juice, sour cream and cream. Cook, stirring, over high heat for 2 minutes.
3 Return pasta to pan, add salmon, chives and almonds and mix well. Cook, stirring, for 1 minute or until heated through. Serve pasta immediately, garnished with extra chopped chives. Serve with a tomato salad.

Chicken and Asparagus Frittata

Preparation time:
  10 minutes
Total cooking time:
  20 minutes
Serves 4

30 g butter
4 spring onions, finely
  chopped
6 eggs, lightly beaten
1 cup milk
2 teaspoons wholegrain
  mustard
1 1/2 cups chopped
  cooked chicken
freshly ground black
  pepper to taste
8 canned asparagus
  spears, drained
3/4 cup grated Swiss
  cheese

1 Heat butter in a large frying pan. Add the spring onions and cook, stirring, for 1 minute or until soft. Whisk together the eggs, milk and mustard.
2 Stir in chicken and pepper to taste. Pour egg mixture over spring onions and cook over low heat for 15 minutes or until frittata is set.
3 Preheat grill. Arrange asparagus on top of frittata and sprinkle with cheese. Place frittata under hot grill for 2 minutes or until cheese is melted and golden. Serve frittata hot or cold with a crisp garden salad.

Chicken and Asparagus Frittata

1. For Chicken and Asparagus Frittata: add spring onions to pan and cook.

2. In a medium mixing bowl, whisk together eggs, milk and mustard.

3. *Pour egg mixture over spring onions and cook over low heat until set.*

4. *Arrange asparagus on the frittata and sprinkle with grated Swiss cheese.*

Salmon and Herb Frittata

Preparation time:
  15 minutes
Total cooking time:
  20 minutes
Serves 4

6 eggs, lightly beaten
1 tablespoon finely
  chopped fresh chives
1/2 cup milk
1/2 cup cream
1 tablespoon finely
  chopped fresh basil
1 tablespoon finely
  chopped fresh dill
1 tablespoon finely
  grated lemon rind
210 g canned red or
  pink salmon
100 g camembert, sliced

1 Whisk eggs, chives,
milk, cream, basil, dill
and rind in large bowl.
Lightly mash salmon;
stir into egg mixture.
2 Pour mixture into a
lightly greased frying
pan. Cook over low
heat for 10–15 minutes
or until almost set.
3 Preheat grill. Top
frittata with slices of
camembert. Place under
preheated hot grill for
2–3 minutes or until
camembert has melted
and frittata is golden.

Herb and Pepper Fettucine

Preparation time:
  10 minutes
Total cooking time:
  20 minutes
Serves 4

400 g fettucine
60 g butter
2 cloves garlic, crushed
2 tablespoons finely
  chopped fresh oregano
2 tablespoons finely
  chopped fresh sage
2 tablespoons finely
  chopped fresh basil
2 teaspoons cracked
  black pepper
1/3 cup freshly grated
  Parmesan cheese

1 Cook the pasta in a
large pan of rapidly
boiling water with a
little oil added until just
tender; drain.
2 Return pan to heat;
add butter. Cook over
medium heat 2 minutes
or until foaming. Add
garlic, oregano, sage,
basil and pepper.
3 Return pasta to pan
to thoroughly combine.
Cook, stirring, for
2 minutes or until pasta
is heated through.
Sprinkle with Parmesan
cheese and serve.

Fettucine with Cheese and Walnut Sauce

Preparation time:
  15 minutes
Total cooking time:
  20 minutes
Serves 4 6

500 g fettucine
1/2 cup white wine
100 g blue cheese,
  crumbled
1/2 cup grated Cheddar
  cheese
1 clove garlic, crushed
1 1/4 cups light sour
  cream
black pepper to taste
1/2 cup chopped
  walnuts or pecans
2 tablespoons walnuts,
  or pecans, extra

1 Cook the pasta in a
large pan of rapidly
boiling water until it is
just tender; drain and
keep warm.
2 Return pan to heat
and add wine, cheeses,
garlic, cream and
pepper to taste. Bring
to boil, reduce heat and
simmer, uncovered, for
5 minutes. Stir in
walnuts or pecans.
3 Divide the pasta
between individual
serving bowls and top
with sauce. Serve
immediately, garnished
with the extra walnuts
or pecans.

---

*Clockwise from top left: Herb and Pepper
Fettucine, Fettucine with Cheese and Walnut
Sauce, Salmon and Herb Frittata*

Cheese and Bacon Omelette

Preparation time:
  10 minutes
Total cooking time:
  10 minutes
Serves 4

4 rashers bacon,
  chopped
4 eggs, lightly
  beaten
1/2 cup milk
1 teaspoon black
  pepper
1/2 teaspoon ground
  nutmeg
30 g butter
2 tablespoons grated
  Cheddar cheese
2 small tomatoes,
  sliced

1 Cook the bacon in a small pan until crisp. Set aside.
2 Whisk together the eggs, milk, black pepper and nutmeg. Heat the butter in an omelette pan over medium heat. Pour in the egg mixture and cook for 4 minutes or until the omelette is set.
3 Sprinkle the cheese on top of the omelette and allow it to melt slightly. Top with the bacon and the sliced tomatoes. Slide out onto a plate and cut into four. Serve with hot buttered toast.

Spaghetti Carbonara

Preparation time:
  5 minutes
Total cooking time:
  15 minutes
Serves 4–6

500 g spaghetti
30 g butter
4 spring onions, finely
  chopped
4 slices leg ham
  (375 g), cut in strips
1 1/4 cups cream
3 eggs, lightly beaten
1/2 cup freshly grated
  Parmesan cheese
1 teaspoon ground
  pepper
2 tablespoons finely
  chopped fresh chives
  or parsley

1 Cook the pasta in a large pan of rapidly boiling water with a little oil added until just tender; drain.
2 Return pan to heat, add butter. Add spring onions and ham. Cook, stirring, 2 minutes. Stir in cream; bring to boil. Reduce heat; simmer, uncovered, 2 minutes.
3 Add beaten eggs, cheese and pepper; mix well. Return pasta to pan. Cook, stirring, over low heat 2 minutes

until heated through. Serve immediately, garnished with chives or parsley.

Spinach Frittata

Preparation time:
  15 minutes
Total cooking time:
  30 minutes
Serves 4

6 eggs, lightly beaten
1 cup milk
250 g packet frozen
  spinach, thawed
1 onion, chopped
1 clove garlic, crushed
1/2 cup grated Cheddar
  cheese
1/2 cup grated
  Parmesan cheese
1 tablespoon finely
  chopped fresh parsley
black pepper to taste

1 Preheat the oven to moderate 180°C. Whisk eggs and milk. Squeeze all water from thawed spinach.
2 Stir spinach, onion, garlic, cheeses, parsley and pepper to taste into the egg mixture.
3 Pour into a greased 23 cm pie plate. Bake for 30 minutes or until set and golden. Serve frittata hot or cold, cut into wedges.

Clockwise from top: Cheese and Bacon Omelette, Spinach Frittata, Spaghetti Carbonara

Seafood Paella

Preparation time:
  30 minutes
Total cooking time:
  30 minutes
Serves 8

2 teaspoons olive oil
250 g pork, chopped
2 small onions,
  chopped
2 cloves garlic, crushed
2 small tomatoes,
  peeled, seeded and
  chopped
2 sticks cabanossi,
  sliced
2 teaspoons olive oil,
  extra
3 cups long-grain rice
3¹/2 cups stock
1 cup white wine
¹/4 teaspoon turmeric
500 g raw prawns,
  peeled, deveined, tails
  left on
500 g mussels, cleaned
2 large calamari hoods,
  cut in thin slices
¹/2 cup frozen peas
salt and freshly ground
  black pepper, to taste

1 Heat oil in a large
pan, add the pork,
onion, garlic, tomato
and cabanossi. Cook,
stirring, for 5 minutes
or until pork is cooked.
Remove from pan and
set aside.
2 Heat extra oil in pan.
Add rice and stir for
1 minute. Add stock
and wine, cover pan
with a tight-fitting lid.
3 Bring slowly to boil;
stir once. Reduce heat,
simmer, covered, for
15 minutes, until liquid
is almost absorbed and
the rice is tender,
adding a little more
liquid if necessary.
4 Add the turmeric,
prawns, mussels, sliced
calamari and peas to
the pan, and simmer
gently for 5 minutes,
stirring occasionally.
Return the pork
mixture to the pan and
heat through. Season
paella with the salt and
black pepper.

Note: Paella originated
as a dish cooked and
eaten out of the pan by
Spanish cattlemen. They
used any ingredients
that were to hand, such
as chicken or seafood,
mixed with rice.

Cheese and Tomato Risotto

Preparation time:
  15 minutes
Total cooking time:
  1 hour 5 minutes
Serves 4

50 g butter
2 onions, chopped
2 cloves garlic, crushed
2¹/2 cups brown rice
1 litre vegetable stock
3 ripe tomatoes,
  chopped
100 g grated Cheddar
  cheese
¹/4 cup grated
  Parmesan cheese
1 tablespoon finely
  chopped fresh herbs
  (eg rosemary, thyme,
  oregano)

1 Melt butter in a large
pan. Add onions and
garlic, cook 5 minutes
or until softened. Add
rice and cook for
2–3 minutes. Pour in
stock, cover and
simmer 45–50 minutes,
until rice is tender. (If
all of the liquid
evaporates and the rice
starts to stick, add a
little more stock.)
2 Stir through the
tomatoes, Cheddar,
Parmesan and herbs.

HINT
Ripe, freshly picked
tomatoes contain
good amounts of
vitamins C and A and
potassium. Hot-house
tomatoes contain only
half the vitamin C of
the fruit grown
outdoors. The vitamin
is concentrated in the
jelly-like substance
surrounding the seeds.

*Seafood Paella (top) and
Cheese and Tomato Risotto*

Spicy Sausage and Bacon Paella

Preparation time:
  20 minutes
Total cooking time:
  45 minutes
Serves 6

4 chorizo or other spicy
  sausages, sliced
  diagonally
4 rashers bacon,
  chopped
1 medium onion, sliced
1 green capsicum, sliced
1 clove garlic, crushed
1 1/2 cups long-grain
  white rice
440 g canned tomatoes
3/4 cup chicken stock
1 teaspoon turmeric
salt and pepper, to taste

1 Cook sausages and
bacon in a large pan
until well browned,
about 5 minutes.
Remove from pan;
drain on paper towels.
2 Add onion, capsicum,
garlic and rice to pan.
Cook over medium
heat, stirring, 3 minutes.
3 Add tomatoes with
juice, chicken stock and
turmeric and stir to
combine. Cover pan
with a tight-fitting lid.
4 Bring slowly to the
boil; stir once. Reduce
heat and simmer,
covered, for 25 minutes
or until the liquid is
almost absorbed and
the rice is tender.
5 Add the sausage and
bacon mixture and heat
through. Season with
salt and pepper.

Chicken Paella

Preparation time:
  30 minutes
Total cooking time:
  1 hour
Serves 4

1/4 cup plain flour
1 teaspoon ground
  black pepper
2 chicken thigh fillets
  (250 g), cut in chunks
3 tablespoons olive oil
2 cloves garlic, crushed
1 medium red or green
  capsicum, chopped
1 large Spanish onion,
  chopped
1 zucchini, sliced
1 cup brown rice
440 g canned tomatoes,
  crushed
2 cups chicken stock
1/2 cup frozen peas
1 tablespoon chopped
  fresh basil
1 tablespoon chopped
  fresh parsley

1 Combine flour and
pepper. Dust chicken in
flour; shake off excess.
2 Heat half the oil in a
pan and cook half of
the chicken quickly
over medium-high heat
until well browned;
remove and drain on
paper towels. Heat the
remaining oil and
repeat the process with
remaining chicken.
3 Add the garlic,
capsicum, onion and
zucchini to the pan.
Cook over medium heat
3 minutes. Stir in the
rice, canned tomatoes
with juice, and stock.
Cover with a tight-
fitting lid.
4 Bring slowly to the
boil; stir once. Reduce
heat and simmer,
covered, for 40 minutes
or until the liquid is
almost absorbed and
the rice is tender.
5 Stir in the peas, fresh
basil, parsley and
chicken, and cook for
5–10 minutes or until
warmed through.

> HINT
> There are two types
> of chorizo sausages
> available. We used
> one similar to salami,
> which just needs
> heating through. It is
> available from good
> delicatessens. The
> other is a fresh
> sausage which needs
> cooking before using.
> It may be purchased
> from good butchers.

*Spicy Sausage and Bacon Paella (top) and
Chicken Paella*

Stir-fry

The short, sharp method and flavours of stir-fry cooking have moved from the kitchens and food stalls of Asia to become a favourite in Western homes. This healthy, extra speedy way of cooking seals in goodness and flavour and is even adaptable to many recipes that did not originate in Asia. Shellfish, firm-fleshed fish, lean meat, poultry and vegetables all work happily in the wok.

Chilli Chicken Stir-fry

Preparation time:
  10 minutes
Total cooking time:
  15 minutes
Serves 2

500 g chicken breast
  fillets
1 tablespoon vegetable
  or peanut oil
8 spring onions, cut into
  4 cm lengths
1 clove garlic, crushed
2 tablespoons tomato
  paste
1/4 cup sweet chilli sauce
1 tablespoon finely
  chopped fresh
  coriander
425 g canned mango
  slices, drained

1 Slice chicken into long, thin strips. Heat oil in a wok or heavy-based frying pan, swirling gently to coat base and sides. Add chicken and stir-fry over high heat for 4 minutes or until well browned and cooked; remove and drain on paper towels.
2 Add spring onions and garlic, stir 1 minute. Add tomato paste, chilli sauce and coriander; stir-fry over high heat for 2 minutes.
3 Return chicken to pan and stir-fry over high heat 1 minute or until heated through. Add mango and gently toss through. Remove from heat and serve with egg noodles.

Chilli Chicken Stir-fry (top) and Chicken with Curry Nut Sauce

Spicy Beef with Snow Peas

Preparation time:
  20 minutes
Total cooking time:
  10 minutes
Serves 4

2 tablespoons soy sauce
1 tablespoon dry sherry
1 tablespoon hoisin
  sauce
1 1/2 teaspoons sugar
1 1/2 teaspoons chilli
  paste
1 tablespoon water
500 g topside steak
2 tablespoons oil
1 teaspoon grated
  ginger
1 clove garlic, crushed
3 carrots, cut in thin
  strips
4 celery sticks, cut in
  thin strips
185 g snow peas

1 tablespoon water
2 teaspoons cornflour

1 Mix together soy sauce, sherry, hoisin sauce, sugar, chilli paste and water. Set aside.
2 Trim meat of fat and sinew. Slice across the grain into long strips. Heat oil in wok or large heavy-based frying pan, swirling gently to coat base and sides. Add half the meat, stir-fry over medium-high heat 2 minutes or until browned; drain on paper towels. Repeat with remaining meat.
3 Add ginger and garlic, stir until golden. Add vegetables, stir-fry over high heat for 2 minutes. Add sauce, mix well. Stir-fry for 2 minutes.
4 Mix together water and cornflour until

smooth. Add to pan; stir-fry until sauce has thickened. Return meat to pan, stir-fry until heated through. Serve with steamed rice.

Beef Stroganoff

Preparation time:
  10 minutes
Total cooking time:
  35 minutes
Serves 6

750 g rump fillet
  steak
1 tablespoon olive oil
2 onions, thinly sliced
500 g button
  mushrooms, sliced
1 cup beef stock
1 tablespoon
  Worcestershire sauce
1 tablespoon tomato
  sauce
1 tablespoon plain flour
1/2 cup light sour cream
black pepper to taste

Spicy Beef with Snow Peas (top) and Beef Stroganoff

3. Add carrots, celery and snow peas and stir-fry over high heat for 2 minutes.

4. Return meat to pan. Stir-fry until heated through.

1 Trim meat of any fat and sinew. Slice across the grain into long, thin strips. Heat oil in a wok or large heavy-based frying pan. Cook meat quickly in small batches over high heat until browned but not cooked through; drain on paper towels.
2 Add onions and mushrooms to pan, stir-fry over high heat for 3 minutes. Return meat to pan with stock and sauces; bring to boil. Reduce heat and simmer, uncovered, for 15 minutes or until meat is cooked.
3 Mix together flour and sour cream until smooth. Add mixture to the pan with pepper, reduce heat and simmer until sauce has thickened. Do not boil. Remove from heat and serve with wholemeal pasta and salad.

Oriental Beef Stir-fry

Preparation time:
  30 minutes
Total cooking time:
  15 minutes
Serves 6

500 g topside or rump
  steak
2 green zucchini
2 yellow zucchini

2 tablespoons oil
150 g sugar snap peas,
  trimmed
250 g button
  mushrooms, sliced
1 red capsicum, sliced
1 green capsicum, sliced
3–4 cups coarsely
  shredded Chinese
  cabbage
8–10 spring onions, cut
  in 5 cm pieces
3 teaspoons cornflour
1 tablespoon water
1 tablespoon oyster
  sauce
1/4 cup soy sauce
2 tablespoons grated
  ginger
1 tablespoon dry sherry
  or sake

1 Trim meat of any fat and sinew. Slice meat across the grain into long, thin strips. Slice the zucchini with a vegetable peeler into long, thin strips. Heat half of the oil in a wok or heavy-based frying pan, swirling gently to coat base and sides. Add half of the meat and stir-fry over high heat for 3 minutes or until well browned. Repeat process with remaining meat. Remove meat from the pan and set aside.
2 Heat remaining oil and add peas, zucchini, mushrooms, capsicum, cabbage and spring onions; stir-fry over high heat for 2 minutes.

3 Mix together the cornflour and water until smooth. Stir in the remaining ingredients. Return meat to pan with sauce mixture and stir-fry over high heat for 3 minutes or until sauce has thickened and beef heated through. Remove from heat and serve immediately with rice noodles.

Lamb and Vegetable Stir-fry

Preparation time:
  15 minutes
Total cooking time:
  15 minutes
Serves 4–6

1/2 cup beef stock
1 tablespoon cornflour
1 tablespoon dry sherry
1 tablespoon soy sauce
1 teaspoon grated
  ginger
1 tablespoon honey
500 g lean lamb
1 tablespoon oil
1/2 cup pine nuts
300 g mushrooms,
  sliced
3 celery sticks, sliced
  diagonally
4 spring onions,
  chopped
125 g frozen peas
1 red capsicum, cut in
  strips
11/2 cups bean sprouts,
  tails removed
(see Note)

Lamb and Vegetable Stir-fry (top) and Oriental Beef Stir-fry

1 Mix together stock, cornflour, sherry, soy sauce, ginger and honey. Set aside.
2 Trim meat of any fat and sinew. Slice across the grain into long, thin strips. Heat some of the oil in a wok or heavy based frying pan. Add half of the meat, stir-fry over high heat until browned; drain on paper towels. Repeat browning process with the remaining meat. Set meat aside.
3 Add the pine nuts and vegetables, except bean sprouts, to pan and stir fry over high heat for 2 minutes.
4 Stir stock mixture, add to pan with bean sprouts, stir-fry over high heat until sauce has thickened. Return meat to pan and stir-fry until heated through. Remove from the heat and serve immediately with pasta or rice.

Note: Bean sprouts should always be cooked very briefly.

Plum Pork and Vegetables

Preparation time:
  10 minutes
Total cooking time:
  20 minutes
Serves 4

1 tablespoon oil
500 g pork fillet
2 small onions, cut in
  wedges
2 teaspoons grated
  ginger
1/2 cup plum jam
2 tablespoons soy sauce
200 g snow peas,
  trimmed
2 small carrots, sliced
  diagonally
2 small parsnips, cut in
  strips

1 Trim meat of any fat and sinew. Slice meat into thin medallions. Heat half of the oil in a wok or heavy-based frying pan, swirling gently to coat base and sides. Add half of the meat and stir-fry over high heat for 4 minutes or until well browned; drain on paper towels. Repeat process with remaining meat.
2 Add onion and ginger and stir-fry over high heat 2 minutes, or until golden. Add jam and soy sauce to pan, stir for 2 minutes or until the jam has melted and thickened slightly.
3 Add snow peas, carrots and parsnips to pan and stir-fry over high heat for 4 minutes. Return meat to pan and stir-fry over high heat for 1 minute, or until heated through.
Remove from heat and serve immediately with Chinese rice noodles.

Coconut Vegetables

Preparation time:
  15 minutes
Total cooking time:
  20 minutes
Serves 4–6

1 tablespoon oil
2 small onions, cut in
  wedges
2 cloves garlic, crushed
1 teaspoon ground
  cumin
1 medium red
  capsicum, chopped
150 g cauliflower
  florets
2 celery sticks, sliced
  diagonally
1 1/2 cups (185 g) grated
  pumpkin
1 cup coconut milk
2 tablespoons sweet
  chilli sauce

1 cup vegetable stock
150 g green beans
1 tablespoon finely
  chopped fresh
  coriander

1 Heat oil in wok or heavy-based frying pan, swirling gently to coat base and sides. Add onion, garlic and cumin; stir for 2 minutes, or until onion is golden.
2 Add the capsicum, cauliflower, celery and pumpkin to pan and stir-fry over high heat for 2 minutes, or until the vegetables have begun to soften.
3 Add the coconut milk, chilli sauce and vegetable stock; bring to the boil. Reduce heat and simmer, uncovered, for 8 minutes, or until the vegetables are almost cooked.
4 Trim tops and tails of beans and cut in half. Add to wok with the coriander, simmer for a further 2 minutes until beans are just tender. Remove from heat and serve immediately with steamed rice.

HINT
Slice vegetables in even-sized pieces on the diagonal or in long, thin strips for stir-frying. The extra surface area means they will cook quickly.

Coconut Vegetables (top) and
Plum Pork and Vegetables

Lime and Seafood Stir-fry

Preparation time:
  20 minutes
Total cooking time:
  15 minutes
Serves 4

500 g *white fish fillets*
12 *large raw prawns*
1 *tablespoon oil*
1 *large calamari tube,*
  cut in 1 cm rings
1 *red capsicum*
10 *stalks fresh*
  asparagus, cut in 5 cm
  lengths
6 *spring onions, sliced*
  diagonally
$^1/2$ *teaspoon ground*
  cumin
1 *tablespoon fresh*
  lemon thyme or 1
  teaspoon dried
2 *teaspoons lime rind*
2 *teaspoons cornflour*
1 *tablespoon water*
2 *tablespoons lime juice*

1 Cut fish fillets into chunks. Peel and devein prawns, leaving the shells intact.
2 Heat half of the oil in a wok or heavy-based frying pan, swirling gently to coat base and sides. Add fish and stir-fry over high heat for 3–4 minutes, or until just cooked. Remove from pan. Heat remaining oil and add prawns and calamari; stir-fry until prawns have just changed colour and calamari is just cooked. Remove from pan.
3 Cut capsicum into strips and add to pan with asparagus, spring onions, cumin, thyme and lime rind. Stir-fry over high heat for 2–3 minutes. Mix cornflour with water and lime juice until smooth.
4 Return seafood to pan with cornflour mixture. Cook 1 minute or until sauce has thickened and seafood has heated through. Remove from heat and serve immediately with crispy fried noodles or fried rice.

Vegetable and Pesto Stir-fry

Preparation time:
  15 minutes
Total cooking time:
  10 minutes
Serves 4

2 *teaspoons oil*
1 *clove garlic, crushed*
1 *red capsicum*
1 *green capsicum*
2 *carrots*
2 *cups shredded cabbage*
1 *small eggplant,*
  chopped
$^1/2$ *cup bottled pesto*
  sauce
$^1/2$ *cup tomato juice*

1 Heat the oil in a wok or heavy-based frying pan, swirling gently to coat the base and sides. Add the crushed garlic and stir for 2 minutes or until golden.
2 Cut the capsicum and carrots into strips and add to the pan with the cabbage and eggplant; stir-fry over high heat for 4 minutes.
3 Stir through pesto and tomato juice and stir-fry 1 minute or until heated through. Remove from heat and serve immediately. Garnish with shavings of Parmesan cheese.

HINT
To make pesto sauce:
Place 1 cup of fresh basil leaves, 2 cloves of crushed garlic, $^1/3$ cup freshly grated Parmesan cheese and $^1/4$ cup pine nuts in food processor and process until finely chopped. With the motor running slowly, add $^1/3$ cup olive oil and process until it forms a smooth paste. Store in jars in refrigerator.

Vegetable and Pesto Stir-fry (top) and
Lime and Seafood Stir-fry

Stir-fry Fish and Vegetables

Preparation time:
  10 minutes
Total cooking time:
  15 minutes
Serves 4

1 tablespoon oil
1 egg, lightly beaten
300 g white fish fillets
1 clove garlic, crushed
1/4 cup frozen peas
2 spring onions, sliced
300 g broccoli florets
1 small red capsicum,
  finely chopped
200 g button
  mushrooms, halved
1 carrot, sliced
2 tablespoons water
1 tablespoon soy sauce
1/2 teaspoon ground
  ginger
pinch five-spice
  powder, optional

1 Heat a little of the oil in a wok or heavy-based frying pan, swirling gently to coat base and sides. Add egg and cook until set. Remove from pan, roll up and slice finely. Set aside.
2 Cut fish into chunks. Add remaining oil to wok and heat, swirling gently to coat base and sides. Add fish and garlic; stir-fry over high heat until flesh has turned white. Remove and set aside.

3 Add the peas, onions, broccoli, capsicum, mushrooms and carrot; stir-fry for 2 minutes.
4 Return fish to wok. Mix together water, soy sauce, ginger and five-spice powder. Return egg slices to the wok with the soy mixture. Stir-fry for 1 minute or until the fish is warmed through. Remove the wok from the heat and serve with steamed rice or noodles.

Creamy Prawn and Tomato Stir-fry

Preparation time:
  10 minutes
Total cooking time:
  15 minutes
Serves 4

750 g medium raw
  prawns
2 teaspoons sun-dried
  tomato oil
4 spring onions, finely
  chopped
1/3 cup sun-dried
  tomatoes, drained and
  cut in strips
1 cup chicken stock
1/2 cup dry white wine
1 cup thickened cream
2 tablespoons finely
  chopped fresh basil

1 Shell and devein prawns. Heat oil in a wok or heavy-based frying pan, swirling gently to coat base and sides. Add prawns and spring onions and stir-fry over high heat for 2 minutes, or until prawns are brightly coloured and cooked. Remove from pan.
2 Add the sun-dried tomatoes, stock, wine and cream to wok; bring to boil. Reduce heat; simmer 7 minutes, or until the sauce has thickened and reduced.
3 Return prawns to wok with basil. Stir-fry over high heat for 1 minute, or until heated through. Remove from heat. Serve with pasta.

HINT
Use tender cuts of meat when stir-frying and trim away all fat and sinew. Suitable cuts of meat to stir-fry include:
Beef: Fillet, topside, rump, blade, round.
Lamb: Tenderloin, fillet, leg strips.
Veal: Loin, rump, fillet, loin chops.
Pork: Leg, fillet, tenderloin, butterfly chops, shoulder.

---

*Creamy Prawn and Tomato Stir-fry and
Stir-fry Fish and Vegetables*

Index